Spi

Lisa Trumbauer

What does a spider look like?

A spider can have
big eyes and little eyes.

A spider can have
a hairy body.

A spider can have
a smooth body.

A spider can have
orange spots.

A spider can have
black and gray stripes.

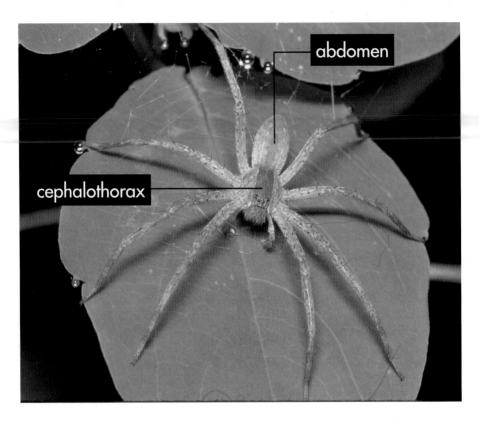

But all spiders
have eight legs
and two body parts.